TRAM
DISASTERS

BRITISH AND FOREIGN TRAM
CRASHES AND ACCIDENTS

Batley, Great Britain, 29 August 1904

In 1904, the Yorkshire Woollen District Electric Tramway saw three tram accidents. In two of them, Car No. 55 was involved: one incident occurred on 16 January, and the other on 29 August, which is illustrated above. In this incident the tram crashed into confectioner George Parrott's horse-drawn van in Purlwell Lane, Batley. Several people were injured though none seriously. Thereafter, car No. 55 was renumbered, becoming car 60.

Amsterdam, Holland, 5 September 1950

Tram No. 263 fails to negotiate a bend and runs into the Amstel on 6 September 1950. (*Photograph by Ben van Meerendonk / AHF, collection International Institute of Social History, Amsterdam*)

TRAM
DISASTERS
BRITISH AND FOREIGN TRAM
CRASHES AND ACCIDENTS

PETER TUFFREY

FONTHILL

Amsterdam, Holland, 17 May 1970
A Renault motor vehicle has collided with a tram on line 17 on 17 May 1970 in Osdorp, Amsterdam. (*Photograph by Henk Graalman*)

Fonthill Media Limited
Fonthill Media LLC
www.fonthillmedia.com
office@fonthillmedia.com

First published 2013

British Library Cataloguing in Publication Data:
A catalogue record for this book is available from the British Library

ISBN 978-1-78155-210-0

Typeset in 9pt on 13pt Sabon
Printed and bound in England

Contents

Acknowledgements   6

Introduction   7

1   British Crashes and Accidents   9

2   Foreign Crashes and Accidents   91

3   British and Foreign Crashes and Accidents in Colour   113

Acknowledgements

I am grateful for help of the following people: Dean Barrow, Roger Benton, David Clay, George Fairley, Gianmarco Giudici, Patrick Glesca, Henk Graalman, Richard Grantham, Darren Hall, David Harvey, Stuart Hastings, Scott Hertel, Peter Jary, Frank De Jong, Peggy Kuo, Paul License, Rene Van Lier, Chico Manobela, Hywel Matthews (Pontypridd Library), Colin Reilly, Ralph Robinson, Jane Salt, State Library of Queensland, Australia, Elaine Shefforth, Alan Sutton, Sue Swatridge, Lucchetti Thomas, Brian Turner.
Special thanks to my son Tristram Tuffrey for his general help behind the scenes.

Every effort has been made to gain permission to use the photographs in this book. If you feel you have not been contacted please let me know: petertuffrey@rocketmail.com

I have taken reasonable steps to verify the accuracy of the information in this book, but it may contain errors or omissions. Any information that may be of assistance to rectify any problems will be gratefully received. Please contact me in writing: Peter Tuffrey, 8 Wrightson Avenue, Warmsworth, Doncaster, South Yorkshire, DN4 9QL.

The Hague, 5 January 2012
Ludovic Hirliman took this picture from his window on the morning of 5 January 2012 in The Hague, South Holland. He said, 'While turning the tram derailed [...] This is affecting three lines, two from htm, number 11 and number 2. One from randstad rail line 4.' Ludovic also filmed the tram being re-railed, and for a time this was on Youtube.

Introduction

I have always been fascinated by trams, just as other people are captivated by racing cars, motorcars, steam locomotives, and buses. I can't explain why, but it all began over thirty years ago when I bought a glass plate photographic collection that depicted, with pin sharp clarity, numerous Doncaster trams. From there I moved on to collecting tram crash postcards and helped Sheffield author Brian Hinchliffe produce a small booklet *Trams in Trouble* in 1990. Since that time, I have collected many more tram crash pictures, and these cover all corners of the globe. Why the fascination with crashes? That's unexplainable too. But disasters hold people's fascination whether they involve aeroplanes, railway engines, fires, explosions etc. So, offering no plausible rational explanations or excuses, this book boldly illustrates tram crashes from the late nineteenth century to the present day.

Many of the British photographs are from picture postcards taken during the heyday of tram operations from 1890 to 1960, when almost every town and city throughout the country relied on this new mode of transport. It is interesting to note that these postcards fetch very high prices today, such is their fascination and rarity. It is also worthy of a mention that a postcard photographer, who had his business premises near where the Exeter crash occurred, was selling views of the incident only an hour later. Pictures of crashes are quite rare, and in several instances, it is acknowledged that a small number are not as good as they should be. But these are probably the only ones that are available.

In my opinion, the most remarkable features of these early postcards are the expressions on the faces of those gathered round the crashed tram – all eager to show their horror of the incident, but all wanting to be included in the picture nonetheless. In certain areas of Lancashire, it is pitiful to observe the clothes some people are wearing, as they are nothing more than rags.

I feature minor collisions to spectacular occurrences. During my research, I came across many, and from different parts of the world, where a motor vehicle has tried to argue with a tram with the inevitable results. This then is perhaps the most common tram accident. More spectacular incidents are illustrated by a crash in Germany, where an aeroplane encountering difficulties landed on a tram. A fortunate occurrence, if indeed it may be described as such, happened in Holland in 1950. A tram, becoming derailed, dashed into a parked car, pushed it into the Amstel and landed on its roof. Quite comically, the driver, who was uninjured, escaped with wet trousers; the water being shallow at that point.

In a large number of cases, as will be gleaned from the text, British crashes were caused through faulty braking systems or driver errors. It is interesting to note that a number of incidents happened during the First World War, and some of these were blamed on the absence of experienced staff.

Once the brakes have failed and the tram is running away down an incline, one of the dilemmas that must have faced passengers was whether or not to jump from the vehicle. During one of the Birmingham crashes, some passengers took it upon themselves to leap from the open top deck of the vehicle. To have that unexpected decision thrust upon a passenger – weighing up which option would cause the least injuries – must have been terrifying.

I read many times in crash reports that medical help at the scene of an incident was sometimes very amateurish, with everyone lending a hand to help to the injured. Victims were treated in local houses, or ferried in anything with wheels to a local hospital.

Thankfully, in some of the more spectacular crashes, at Scarborough and Ramsgate, where trams have fallen substantial distances, the passengers only suffered slight injuries. Many people in numerous accidents were reported as suffering shock, and it can only be imagined how they coped thereafter. The mental scars must have stayed with them forever.

For the most part, I have steered away from all the technical aspects surrounding the causes of a crash and tried to deal with the more human and social elements. Where possible, names of drivers and conductors have been included, along with tragic, bizarre, and in rare cases humorous elements of an incident.

In recent years, it is remarkable that we have seen the re-introduction of trams around the world. Unfortunately, this has brought a new era of tram crashes, and I have tried to include several of these, ie. Dublin and Sheffield. But this new era has not produced tram crash postcards. Instead, crashes are now largely featured on the internet; at the present time on Youtube, where all types of collisions may be viewed.

I made many requests to private individuals, public libraries and societies for information concerning the crashes, and the response was marvellous, helpful, and courteous. Quite a number of contacts have been made throughout the world to compile the Foreign b/w and colour sections. In Holland, I am particularly grateful to the assistance received from Frank de Jong and Henk Graalman. Their help has been invaluable. And it has to be said that some of the most spectacular and tragic pictures of crashes came from them. Henk Graalman, who now lives in Australia, provided not only pictures taken in Holland, but his new country of residence.

Many foreign b/w and colour pictures were acquired from Flickr users, and almost without exception, the response from these people was amazing, many going out of their way to help with the project. They have also supplied invaluable information about the crashes. Some individuals were even on a fated vehicle, or in the immediate vicinity when a particular incident occurred.

In certain instances, trams also suffered destruction from enemy aerial action during the Second World War, and I have felt that dramatic pictures of these incidents has warranted them being included in the book. Large numbers of trams were destroyed, as can be seen in Britain in the pictures of Abbey Wood and Clapham depots. I have even sneaked in a picture of a tram in Sunderland destroyed in enemy action during the First World War.

Regardless of whether the reader is interested in trams, or disasters of any type, I feel this book has a wealth of interest for those interested in the changing social and transport scene over the last 100 years or more.

CHAPTER 1

British Crashes and Accidents

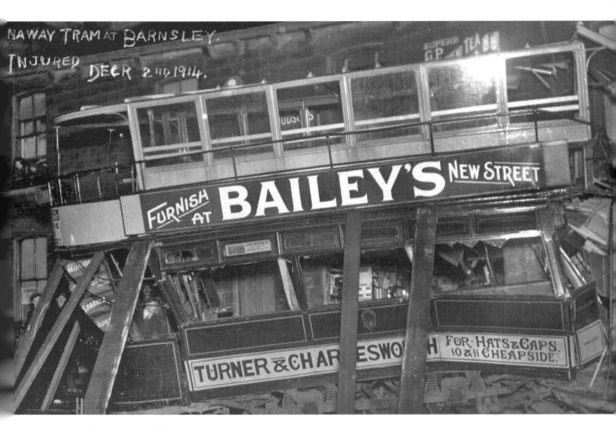

Barnsley, 2 December 1914

The mishap occurred about 4.30 p.m. on 2 December 1914 on what was known as the Old Mill route, from the town's Midland Railway Station to the Gas Works, where the gradient from Eldon Street is very steep. Car no. 4, belonging to the Barnsley & District Light Railway, had been stationary but started while the driver was off the platform; it ran down the incline, a distance of a full quarter of a mile, gaining speed. The car kept the rails until reaching the curve near the Prince of Wales Hotel when it jumped the metals and dashed across the road into the shop of J. C. Dodd, general dealer, completely wrecking the front. Willing helpers were speedily at work helping the injured, who were taken as quickly as possible to the Beckett Hospital. The conductor of the car, John Priestley, was on the vehicle when it started and he made efforts to apply the brake, but failing to pull the car up, he, along with some of the passengers, managed to jump off before it crashed into the shop. Only six people were travelling on the tram at the time; all were injured, two fatally.

Opposite above: Bath

In Wells Road, Bath, on 3 July 1933, there was a collision between two cars numbered 6 and 18. Open top car No. 6, belonging to the Bath Electric Tramways, with forty passengers on board, ran backwards down a hill and collided with car No. 18, also carrying many passengers. On impact, the two cars travelled for around 150 yards before coming to a halt. Car No. 6, which was travelling from the centre of the town into one of the suburbs on the hillside, gathered pace despite the frantic efforts of the driver who remained at his post. The driver of the second car, seeing that a crash was inevitable, jumped clear. Two ambulances, private cars and lorries were used to take the injured to hospital. There were two deaths (on car No. 6) and thirty-seven injuries in total. The drivers and conductors of both vehicles escaped with minor injuries. Because it was an extremely hot day, it was reported that problems caused by melted tar on the track had indirectly been responsible for car No. 6 to roll backwards.

Opposite below: Batley, 16 January 1904

The scene at Batley on 16 January 1904.

Above: Batley, 16 January 1904

An accident occurred on the Yorkshire Woollen District Electric Tramways on Saturday afternoon 16 January 1904. What was known as the Thorncliffe Road section began at the bottom of Hick Lane in Batley and terminated in a junction at Halifax Road, Stancliffe, with the British Electric Traction Co's Spen Valley system. A few minutes before 4 p.m., driver Walter Dawer started car No. 55 from Thorncliffe Road end for Batley. Only a few passengers were inside the car. It was noticed that the tram was running at great speed along the straight piece of track in Thorncliffe Road – much too fast indeed to 'negotiate' the corner in Track Road. Dawer applied the handbrake with force, but it was too late. The car left the rails and went across the road, forcing it through a stone wall (6 feet high) that skirted the garden of the residence of Mark Oldroyd, ex-MP for Dewsbury. The entire body of the car was left standing among the shrubs, and the driver lay among the stones and broken glass. The front of one side of the car was completely wrecked. The car remained in Mr Oldroyd's garden for several days, and a great number of people visited the scene of the accident. No loss of life occurred; several passengers and the driver suffered cuts and bruises.

Birmingham, 1 October 1907

On Tuesday morning 1 October, 1907, double-decker tram No. 22, carrying workmen, was on the outskirts of Birmingham when it ran down a hill in Warstone Lane and overturned on a sharp curve at the bottom. There were approx. twenty men on board. Some jumped from the top of the car when it left the rails, and others were flung into the street when it overturned. The cause of the accident was attributed to the mishandling of the car by an inspector who had boarded shortly before the accident happened. Two people were killed and others were injured.

Birmingham, 26 June 1916

On 26 June 1916, double-decker car No. 46, belonging to the South Staffordshire Tramway Co., was travelling on a service between Colmore Row in Birmingham and Darlaston. Outside Soho Station in Soho Road, Handsworth, the tram failed to enter a loop and turned over.

 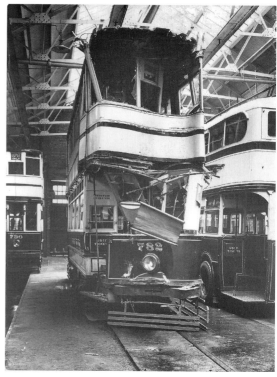

Above, left and right: **Birmingham, December 1935**

A view taken inside Washwood, Wood Heath Garage, showing damage to Birmingham City Transport vehicles No. 782 and 776. They collided at the junction of Saltley Road and Nechells Place on 12 December 1935. Some road works were being undertaken near the junction, and the track was reduced to a section of single line working. Car 782 was waiting for car 791 to pass through the road works when it was hit at some speed from behind by 776. 782 was pushed forward into the oncoming 791. All three trams were damaged, with 776 and 782 coming off worse. Around sixty-five passengers received minor injuries. Photographs from the Jim Sheldon Collection.

Opposite: **Blackburn, 20 September 1941**

Darwen Corporation double-decker Car No. 17 was involved in an accident at Blackburn at around 1.00 p.m. on 20 September 1941. The car was working the 12.52 p.m. ordinary service from Blackburn to Darwen along Bolton Road, and was travelling through the facing points leading to the Kidder Street football traffic siding when it was wrongly diverted into that area. The car was derailed on the sharp left-handed curve immediately following the points, and the body left the bogies and overturned on its right-hand side. Motorman R. Webb was pinned under the overturned body and killed instantly. Coming to Darwen from London, he had been with the service for eighteen years. The conductor John House escaped with bruises and a shaking. People from neighbouring houses rushed to the scene to give assistance, and ambulances and an A.R.P. rescue vehicle were brought into service. There were about twenty-four passengers in the car, distributed almost equally between the upper and lower decks; of these, thirteen were taken to hospital with cuts from broken glass and bruises, but only three were detained. Mr J. W. Sykes, the occupier of the shop whose gable end the tram crashed, said afterwards that he was resting in bed when the accident happened. 'I heard it take the bend and knew it had missed the points,' he said, 'and as I scrambled out of bed it crashed into the house below my bedroom.'

The body of the car was not crushed, but suffered considerable damage on the right-hand side, and the upper saloon was partly broken away from the lower.

Opposite: **Blackburn, 20 September 1941**

Two more views of car No. 17 after the crash in Kidder Street. The *Northern Daily Telegraph* of Saturday 13 December 1941 gave details of Major G. R. S. Wilson's report on the accident: 'His findings are that the accident was primarily due to the open position of the switch tongue concerned, following the failure of the means adopted to secure it for the straight. The statements of Motormen Couple (of Darwen) and Pickard (of Blackburn) as to its position before the accident were 'conflicting', and in his opinion neither man's evidence was altogether reliable. He thought however, it was probably the rubber securing block was not in place during the morning and that the vibration of passing trams and other road traffic caused the tongue to work open gradually.'

Wilson also recommended that some positive mechanical arrangement should be adopted 'to secure these and other facing points' on the system when not regularly used, and 'the Blackburn Corporation should be asked to report what action they proposed'.

Above: **Bolton, February 1941**

People trapped under seats, which had broke loose from their fittings, were among 40 passengers treated for injuries at Bolton Royal Infirmary on 12 February 1941 after a collision between two tramcars. The accident happened just before two-o'clock on the Tonge Moor route in Folds Road, near the Bank Street – Bow Street junction. Both trams were thrown off the rails. One of the cars, travelling uphill, was leaving a length of single track, and the other was entering it, when the collision occurred. Passengers screamed as the car going downhill shed its wheels and toppled over against a tram standard. The car was almost completely wrecked. The back wheels of the other car left the rails, but it remained upright and was only slightly damaged. Fortunately neither tram was heavily loaded. Passers-by helped to rescue people from the wrecked car, and those who were trapped were released within a few minutes. The driver of the outward bound tram was Henry Blackledge and the conductor, Bert Fowler; of the inward bound tram C. Smith and E. Sutcliffe respectively. None of these staff members were listed among the injured.

THE WRECKED TRAM CAR, BOURNEMOUTH MAY 1ST 190

Above: **Bournemouth, 1 May 1908**

Bournemouth Corporation Tramways served the town of Bournemouth in Dorset from 23 July 1902 until 8 April 1936. One of Britain's worst tram disasters occurred in the town on 1 May 1908 when seven people were killed and twenty-six injured. Double deck car No. 72 was travelling from Westbourne to Christchurch when at the top of Commercial Road, where an incline began, it was noticed to be going faster than usual. The car failed to pull up at the statutory stopping place and went round a bend across what was known as 'the Triangle' at a rapid rate. On turning into Avenue Road, the vehicle was seen to be running on the side wheels, and some of the passengers, becoming greatly alarmed, jumped off. A little further down, the car left the rails, and swerving to the left, dashed through the railings of the grounds of a house called Fairlight Glen. Here there was a drop of from 15 to 20 feet, and the car completely overturned into the garden below, which immediately abutted on the Central Pleasure Grounds. There were from thirty-five to forty passengers on the car at the time, most of whom were on the top, and in overturning, the car fell on to some of them. The driver, named Wilton, and the conductor, Finch, who both stuck to their posts, were badly shaken, but not seriously injured. The car itself was completely wrecked.

Opposite: **Bournemouth, 1 May 1908**

A postcard view of the Bournemouth crash, published by W. Gothard of Barnsley.

Bournemouth, 1 May 1908
An inspector looking into the full details surrounding the tragedy attributed much of the blame to poor maintenance procedures and shoddy organisation at management level.

Bradford, 4 December 1889
An accident happened at Four Lane Ends, Allerton, on the Bradford Tramways & Omnibus Co's system on 4 December 1889. The *Yorkshire Post* of 5 December 1889 reported that the tramway accident that occurred at Allerton near Bradford on Wednesday: 'Has resulted in the death of one person and injury to several others. It appeared that by some means the car became detached from the engine when operating from Bradford to Allerton, and ran back down an incline until on reaching a curve it left the rails and fell on its side. Of the people in the car when it began running back several escaped unhurt or with very slight injuries; but nine were in the car when it fell over and of these one man was killed and the others received injuries, in four cases of a serious nature.'

Bradford, 31 July 1907

Bradford Corporation car. No. 210, descending one of the steepest of the inclines leading into the centre of Bradford, got out of control on the morning of 31 July 1907, and in the collision with a building that stopped its course approx. thirteen people were injured. The accident occurred about 6 a.m. when the car was nearing the city on its second journey from Undercliffe to Saltaire. The city's steepest gradient is in Church Bank, which leads into Forster Square, and here for a 100 yards or so it is as much as 1 in 9 to 1 in 10. It was at this point that the accident occurred. Speedily, there were plenty of willing workers to assist in releasing the passengers, many of whom were practically imprisoned in the wreckage. In some cases, woodwork had to be broken so they could be released. The driver escaped with minor injuries, as did the conductor, but a passerby was severely injured, resulting in his leg being amputated. The accident was the result of the front axle snapping.

Bradford, 1 February 1918

Allerton stands high above the level of the centre of Bradford, and the tramway route was very steep from the end of Chapel Lane. Not only was the gradient steep for around a mile, but at the point where it became less severe, there was an acute angle. It was at this point, in the early hours of 1 February 1918, that an accident occurred involving car No 88. It resulted in the death of driver W. Gill and injuries to twenty passengers. Curiously, the same car some five years earlier was blown over at the top of Allerton in a gale, and at that time, Gill, who had been a driver for about sixteen years, was in charge of it.

Burnley, 21 December 1923

Two people were killed and at least another five were injured in a tram accident at Burnley on 21 December 1923. The mishap was the result of a collision between Burnley Corporation car No. 10 and a lorry. The car had reached the top of a steep incline when the front portion was struck by the skidding lorry. The impact put the brake apparatus out of control and the tram rushed down the hill. For about 150 yards the track was reasonably straight, but at the bottom of the incline there was a bend in the road leading from Briercliffe Road to Lane Head, and there the car, after coming into contact with a post, left the rails and crashed into a newsagent's shop. The driver and conductor stuck to their posts while the car was running away. The driver William Norris was badly injured, and the conductor William Simpson was so seriously hurt that he died in hospital an hour after the accident.

Burton-upon-Trent, 8 October 1919

The conductress and a passenger died as a result of a tram accident on the Burton & Ashby Light Railway on 8 October 1919. About twenty others were hurt, half a dozen seriously. Car No. 18 was travelling up Bearwood Hill Road, the steepest road in Burton, when it stopped and then started to run back. Driver Charles Insley tried vainly to hold it with the brakes, and the conductress Lilian Parker applied the sand pedal. But the car dashed away at speed, and at the bottom jumped the metals, being thrown on its side partly in the grounds of River House, within a few yards of the River Trent. The driver and the conductress stuck to their posts to the end, and the conductress was found pinned under the car and died as a result of her injuries. Some passengers attempted to leave the car, but all on the top were scattered on the road. The inside passengers suffered most, being imprisoned amid flying glass and wreckage.

Darwen, 20 September 1926
Two people were killed and seven injured when car No. 11, travelling from Hoddleston to Darwen at 6.25 a.m. on 20 September 1926, got out of control when descending Sudell Road, Darwen. It crashed into the front of a billards hall in Bridge Street, wrecking the premises. The car was almost smashed to pieces. At the time of the crash, a severe thunderstorm was raging.

Opposite: **Darwen, 20 September 1926**
Driver William Alston escaped, suffering from severe shock. The car was a 'workmen's', and fortunately was only carrying a few passengers. The accident was put down to driver error combined with adverse weather conditions and an ineffective braking system on the tram.

Above: **Devonport, 27 November 1914**
A serious accident occurred shortly after 7 a.m. on Friday 27 November 1914 on the Devonport & District tramway system, a car overturning at the bottom of a steep incline and resulting in three people being killed and approx. thirty-three injured. The accident happened at the bottom of the hill leading from St Michael's Terrace to the Technical School, and the car No. 25 was a special one, used for conveying workmen who had been on a night shift in the North Yard, Devonport, to Penneycomequick and district. A large number of workmen boarded the tram at the North Gates, and at Keyham Gates, the number was further increased. It was stated that the car was overcrowded both inside and out. Alfred Cheek was the driver, and he made desperate attempts to stop the car running out of control. But his efforts were fruitless, and as the tram reached the bottom of the hill, it jumped the rails and overturned, the front part eventually being brought up against the stone wall that formed the boundary of the road leading to the London & South Western Station. A number of the inside passengers, realising the dangerous speed at which the car was travelling down the hill, jumped off before it overturned. The passengers who did not manage to escape fared the worst. Plenty of help was soon at hand, and amongst the first on the scene was a number of St John Ambulance men from the military hospital nearby. The driver was taken to hospital, but his injuries were not considered serious and he was allowed home shortly afterwards. The same happened to the conductor William Riley. The scene of the accident was exactly the same spot where a similar accident occurred around fourteen years earlier, when a passenger riding on the outside of the tram that ran down the hill and jumped the rails was killed.

Dewsbury, 20 May 1904

Just before 3 p.m. on Friday 20 May 1904, double-decker car No. 6, which had come from Heckmondwike via Staincliffe, was travelling towards Dewsbury when the driver Walter Stead lost control of the vehicle. Inside the car were five or six passengers. One man jumped out, suspicious that all was not well. The others were instructed by the conductor to keep their places. Gathering momentum, the car collided against the wheel of a mineral water cart, ripping off the tyre and spokes, and scattering bottles and boxes everywhere. Stead was knocked off the footboard on to the road and driverless the car went on. It came into contact with a fully laden coal cart, and a good deal of the coal was thrown into a confectioners window. The curious mixture of 'black-diamonds' and pastry attracted many spectators. The driver of the cart was knocked down, but escaped serious injury. These two collisions slightly checked the flight of the car, and at the entrance to the market place it ran into a chemical manufacturer's dray laden with empty carboys. Just beyond were two other tram cars, one destined for Ravensthorpe and the other for Birkenshaw. All the time the runaway had kept to the metals. It now jumped the points, collided with the first two of the cars mentioned, and the conductor was badly hurt. The two stationery cars were driven one against the other, and as the runaway had now reached a level piece of road, the force of the impact brought it to a standstill. Very much shaken, but not seriously hurt, the passengers got out and were able to go their separate ways. Two car conductors were injured, and the cars damaged. In a report on the event, it was recommended that drivers needed more training before operating tram cars.

Dewsbury, 12 October 1915

A crash occurred at Dewsbury on 12 October 1915. Car No. 3 – running light – was driven by John Callaghan for the National Electric Construction Company, which had powers to run between Dewsbury, Ossett, and Earlsheaton. It left the metals at the terminus in front of Dewsbury Town Hall and crashed into Hilton's shop, adjoining the Scarborough Hotel. Tuesday afternoon was a half day for Dewsbury traders and their assistants, and it was fortunate that there was no one on the premises, or the result might have been more serious.

Dewsbury, 12 October 1915

The driver jumped off the car 10 yards before it came in contact with the building, and the conductress Maggie Sadler also tried to escape, but both were injured. The front portion of the car smashed through the wall of the shop and was embedded inside it. An hour later, the room above, occupied as a drawing room and a billiard saloon, suddenly collapsed and fell on to the car and into the market place. Damage to the building, contents, and car was estimated between £2,000

and £3,000. A Mrs Pinder and her daughter Mrs Noble were injured by a horse and cart that was getting out of the way of the car. All four people were taken to Dewsbury District Infirmary. From statements made by several eye-witnesses, it would appear that it was owing to the greasy state of the metals, through the rain, that the driver lost control of the car about 100 yards from the terminus. This was the third accident that had occurred in the same locality since the line opened.

Doncaster, 21 October 1920

For several hours on Thursday 21 October 1920, the tramway service between Doncaster and Brodsworth was interrupted after a collision between a Doncaster Corporation tramcar and a powerful traction engine. The consequences of the smash might have been much more serious, as there were a fair number of passengers travelling on the tram, but apart from being shaken, no-one was injured. The tractor, belonging to Messrs Edwards & Co. of Doncaster, was travelling from Doncaster with a couple of wagons. It met the tram about midway between the railway bridge, near the Sprotbrough Road turning and the Sun Inn, at a point where the road was narrow. There was a fog at the time, which must have prevented either of the drivers from seeing far ahead, and the noise of the approaching tractor or car seems to have been deadened to the drivers by the noise of their own vehicles.

Opposite: Dover, 19 August 1917

On 19 August 1917, the Dover to River branch of the Dover Corporation Electric Tramways experienced the worst tram accident ever seen in Britain. Eleven people were killed with fifty-nine injured. The incident occurred on the steep incline from Crabble Hill to the athletic ground. Open top, double-decker car No. 20 got out of control, and crashed into a wall at the foot of the hill with such force that it was slewed round and crashed over on to its side.

Dover, 19 August 1917

The Dover car was crowded with passengers who were taking a trip to the river. Driver Bressenden jumped off the car and escaped with minor injuries. The section of line where the disaster occurred had been opened for a number of years, and this was the first accident of any kind that had occurred.

Dudley, 29 November 1920

Single-decker car No. 77, belonging to the Dudley, Stourbridge & District Traction Company, was involved in an incident on Castle, Hill Dudley, on 29 November 1920. Skidding and leaving the metals adjacent to Dudley Opera House, the car collided with a lorry, and mounting the pavement, crashed partially through a railway over bridge. Both the driver and conductor, along with fourteen passengers, escaped with shock and minor injuries. They were all very lucky, as beyond the bridge there was a 60 feet drop. Driver Frank Richards was praised for staying with the car, but an official report stated he should have been more aware of speed restrictions in this particular area shortly before the mishap.

Edinburgh, 6 April 1936
Edinburgh Corporation double-decker car No. 206 collided with a traction engine on 6 April 1936.
Several passengers were injured in the accident.

Exeter, 7 March 1917
Whilst travelling from Heavitree to Dunsford Hill on 7 March 1917, driver Charles Saunders lost
control of Exeter car No. 12 as it started to descend the 1 in 11 hill of Fore Street. The car collided
with a horse and cart – killing the horse – and subsequently left the rails and turned on its side,
hitting the parapet of a bridge before coming to a halt. The conductress jumped off the car before
the crash and suffered shock and minor injuries. One of the five passengers on board was killed.
The driver and two of the passengers were seriously hurt. The tram was badly damaged. On www.
exetermories.co.uk, it is stated: 'The photographic studio of Henry Wykes overlooked the bridge at
that time, so he was soon on the spot recording the accident with his camera. Within an hour he
was selling postcards from his studio door of the disaster.'

Gateshead, 5 February 1916

On Saturday night 5 February 1916, four people were killed in a crash at Gateshead. Car No. 7 started on its journey from the Bensham terminus in Saltwell Road, and after rounding a sharp curve from Saltwell Road to Bensham Road, it travelled about 200 yards up the steep hill known as Bensham Bank. It then reached a loop, where a down car was to pass it, but the down car appeared to be stuck at the loop above. After ringing his bell several times without the down car moving, the driver of the up car Leonard Jane set his brakes to hold his car and went up the hill towards the other one. More passengers got on the up car in the meantime, and the car began to move backwards. Considerable speed was gathered in the 200 yards run back to the right-angled turn into Saltwell Road, and the car failed to take the turn, overturning on to waste ground. All the passengers escaped with their lives; the four killed being pedestrians who were passing at the time and could not get out of the way quickly enough.

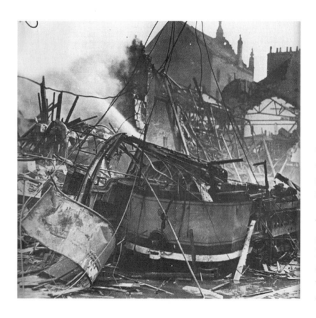

Glasgow, 17 March 1941

Glasgow Standard No. 6 suffered bomb damage in Nelson Street, Glasgow, on 17 March 1941. Glasgow Corporation Transport was allowed to build a replacement car for Standard No. 6 on the grounds that it was destroyed by enemy action. There was also insurance money from the destruction of the car.

Glasgow, 18 May 1931

On 18 May 1931, a Glasgow car was travelling at speed along Dumbarton Road when it jumped the points at the Scotstoun Emporium. The motorman was thrown under the front bogie and killed. Artist Achille Beltrame (1871-1945) produced a picture of the crash for the front cover of an Italian magazine *La Domenica del Corriere*, 14 June 1931.

Glasgow, June 1939

Phase III/2 car No. 869 was involved in a mishap in June 1939 at the corner of Kenmure Street and Albert Drive in Pollokshields. It was working on route No. 3. The car was not repaired, but scrapped in the same month.

Opposite above: **Bilsland Drive, Glasgow, May 1947**
Crash scene on Bilsland Drive - where it curves sharply under the canal bridge - in May 1947 involving Phase 1 Standard car No. 643. Thereafter, the tram's lower deck was retained and it was rebuilt with a new top deck.

Opposite below: **Glasgow Hyndland, *c.* 1940**
This accident involving Phase III Standard car. No. 151 occurred on the west side of a railway bridge at the foot of Clarence Drive in Hyndland *c.* 1940. As a result of the damage, the car was scrapped in May 1940.

Above, left and right: **Great Orme, 23 August 1932**
Two people were killed and about twenty holidaymakers injured on Tuesday 23 August 1932 when car No. 4, working on the cable tramcar service operated on the Great Orme, Llandudno, got out of control. The 'draw bar', to which the cable was attached to the tram, snapped, and the car dashed down the incline, crashing over a steep part of the Great Orme to hit a wall, hurling the occupants in all directions. The tramway was operated by cables that were worked by engines in a power house half way up Great Orme. Margaret Worthington, the daughter of one of the tramway employees, had taken her father's dinner to the winding shed, and she was riding with the driver in front of the tram on her return journey. Realising the danger, Harris, the driver, picked up the girl and jumped. Unfortunately, he jumped the wrong side of the tram and they were both killed. (*Photographs courtesy of Jim Payne*)

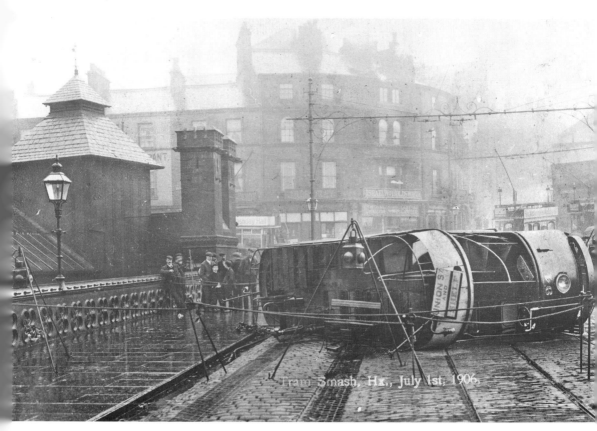

Tram Smash, Hx., July 1st, 1906.

Opposite above: Halifax, 1 July 1906
The tram disaster at Halifax on Sunday evening 1 July 1906 did not occur on the worst gradient
of the town's tramway system, but on the incline – the gradient was 1 in 16 – known as New Bank
on the Shelf route. Shortly after 7 p.m., car No. 94, driven by Theodore Chadwick, was descending
this thoroughfare, when as he applied the brakes, he noticed that they failed to 'bite', the rails being
'greasy'. The car gained speed, and despite the efforts of the driver and conductor William Duffey,
both of whom remained at their posts throughout, it quickly got beyond control. When the runaway
car reached North Bridge, it jumped the points, but it continued running along the bridge for 20
or 30 yards before it crashed, turning over on its right side. The total number of passengers outside
and inside the car was fifteen, and all of these sustained injuries; two were killed. A report on the
incident apportioned part of the blame on Chadwick's misuse of the car's braking system during
inclement weather conditions.

Opposite below: Halifax, 15 July 1917
One person was killed and thirty-seven others injured when the Queensbury-Halifax tram No. 99
overturned at Ambler Thorn on 15 July 1917.

Above: Halifax, 22 May 1915
Halifax Corporation Tramways car No. 89 overturned at Lee Bridge, Halifax, on Saturday evening
22 May 1915. The two-decker car was running between Overnden, Halifax, and Savile Park.
During the accident, windows were smashed and passengers were pitched violently against each
other. The driver Henry Armitage escaped almost unhurt, but his conductor J. Sutcliffe suffered
injuries to his face and head. The car was carrying approx fifty-six passengers, and some of them
scrambled out of the car, but others who were more seriously injured had to be assisted out. Help
was quickly forthcoming, and doctors and ambulance men summoned by telephone arrived on the
scene. Some of the passengers had been cut by the broken glass and others were suffering from
internal injuries. They were carried into adjoining houses, and after first aid had been given were
taken to the local infirmary, some in ambulance carriages and others in motorcars and taxi cabs. A
few of the injured passengers were taken direct to their own homes, where they received medical
attention, and a number of others whose injuries were comparatively slight were able to walk home.
The accident was attributed to poor maintenance of track and tram.

TRAM ACCIDENT
BRADLEY
NEAR HUDDERSFIELD

Above: Bradley, Huddersfield, 22 April 1905

There was a mishap on the Huddersfield Corporation tram system on 22 April 1905. At 7.40 a.m., car No. 26 left the top of Northumberland Street, with driver Matthew Smith and conductor John Earnshaw. The car travelled satisfactorily as far as the Woodman Inn, Bradley, and there were no passengers when it left that point for the terminus opposite the White Cross Inn, Bradley. That section of the journey was down hill, and it was said that the driver lost control of the car through the brakes not acting. The conductor was thrown off the platform on to the road. The driver kept at his post until the car reached the terminus and ran off the end of the rails. Then, he went through the car to the rear and jumped off. The car ran down the road, but turned to the left and dashed through the garden wall of a private residence where it broke down a large tree, stripped off large branches of others, and came to a halt about 150 yards from the terminal rails. When the driver jumped off, he was badly hurt; the conductor was severely shaken and injured an arm.

Opposite above: Bradley, Huddersfield, 22 April 1905

Another view of the incident at Bradley, Huddersfield, 22 April 1905.

Opposite below: Huddersfield, 6 June 1905

Huddersfield Corporation tram No. 67, on its way from Lindley to Huddersfield during the evening of 6 June 1905, got out of the control of driver J. Woffenden when going down Holly Bank Road, a steep gradient. It left the metals at the curve of the main road and crashed through a 4 feet wall into a field belonging to J. H. Kaye. The driver escaped without serious injury and the conductor suffered slight injuries to his knees. There were a few passengers in the car, and they escaped with a severe shaking.

TRAM ACCIDENT
BRADLEY
NEAR HUDDERSFIELD   APRIL 22/05

"RUNAWAY CAR"
EDGERTON JUNE 6TH/05.

MARSH LINDLEY

USE HOLLOWAY'S PILLS & OINTMENT

Reckitt's BLUE.

CHH　　TRAM ACCIDENT NEWSOME　　SAT MAR 3ᵈ 1906.　　B

Huddersfield, 3 March 1906

At about 1.15 p.m on Saturday 3 March 1906, Huddersfield Corporation Tramways car No. 26 was working on an outward journey to Newsome Road, and was brought to a standstill at Malvern Road. On the driver Albert Spencer throwing off the brake, the car failed to start. It moved backwards down the hill and gathered momentum; the brakes being applied without any effect. The tram travelled at speed along the bridge spanning the River Colne and left the line at the sharp curve into Colne Road, crossed the road in the direction of a chip shop, and then on to waste land adjoining. Here, a greengrocer's horse and cart had been left standing. The car collided with the cart; the shafts were broken off, the axle smashed, and the horse – freed from its harness – ran off. The passengers, who had no opportunity of escaping, were severely shaken, and several of them received other injuries.

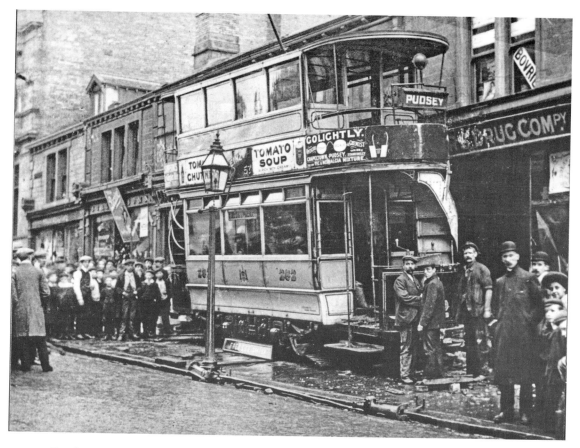

Leeds, 8 September 1909

As the 5.20 a.m. Tram No. 282 from Pudsey to Leeds was going down Church Lane, Pudsey, on Wednesday 8 September 1909, the brakes failed to act. The car travelled until it reached the sharp curve near Pudsey Town Hall, when it left the rails and continued down Lowtown. Driver Herbert Woodall remained at his post until he realised that it was hopeless to stop the car. It left the road, mounted the pavement, and was heading for the shops on the north side of the street. Woodall however, managed to turn it broadside on, lessening the force of the impact. Yet two shop fronts, F. Coe's and Taylor's Drug Stores, were badly damaged. The passengers in the car, which was a workman's, suffered shock. One man hurt his knee in jumping off the vehicle; another sustained a fractured rib. Woodall escaped with slight injuries. It was some hours before the disabled car could be removed from the pavement.

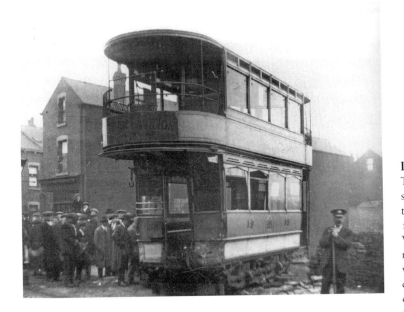

Leeds, 13 June 1916
The Leeds tramway system saw an accident during the morning of 13 June 1916 in Oldfield Lane, Wortley, Leeds. It was the result of a hopper tramway vehicle breaking away and colliding with a passenger car. Several people were seriously injured. The hopper car had taken a load of clay from the Leeds Fireclay Company's pits at Harehills to the company's works at Upper Wortley. After the trolley pole had been reversed for the return journey, a workman, thinking that the driver was at his post on the front platform, released the brake at the rear. However, before the driver could get to his station, the car moved off down a slope. It encountered nothing to check its high speed for a distance of over a mile – all down hill – until the collision occurred in Oldfield Road. It crashed into car No. 19 running from Lower Wortley to the Corn Exchange. The passenger car was hurled forward, and then both trams jumped the metals. The passenger vehicle swerved sharply to the left and went across the pavement through a wall 4 or 5 feet high and half way into a field. The other tram remained on the road.

Leeds, 18 September 1916.

About 4.40 p.m. on 18 September, Leeds tram No. 281, which was travelling down the steep incline of Richardshaw Lane from Pudsey to Leeds, left the rails where there was a sharp curve near the Sun Hotel, and ran across the road into the shop window of Fred Coe, draper and clothier. It was understood that Herbert Allsop was learning to drive at the time, and he was accompanied by George Hirst, who was an experienced driver. One woman suffered a back injury.

Leeds, 12 May 1923

Seven people were killed and forty-four injured in a tramway accident that happened on the Morley route of the Leeds Tramways at about 7 a.m. on Saturday 12 May 1923. A workman's tramcar (No. 191) from Morley to Leeds ran away down Churwell Hill, and at speed jumped the rails at the bottom, dashed into a wall, and overturned in the road. Although the tram was not as full as it might have been on an ordinary week day, it was carrying about fifty people on board, many of whom worked at Messrs Ingle, tanners and curriers, and Messrs George Hepworth & Sons dyers. There were also travellers to Leeds, and many of the passenger were women and girls. The driver was not with the car. It was said that he had been thrown off or had made a wild leap for safety coming down the hill. It was found that a number of factors contributed to the accident, including bad maintenance and staff errors.

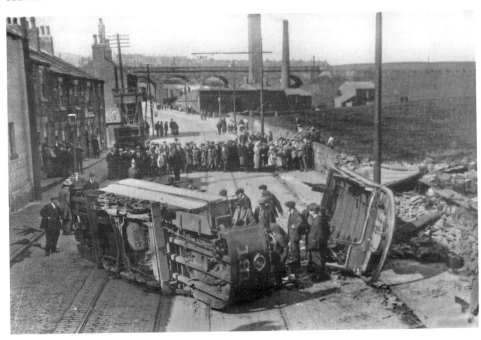

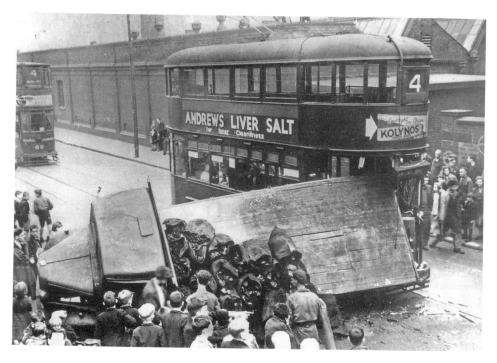

Leeds, 2 October 1945
On 2 October 1945, car no. 458 collided with a coal truck in Kirkstall Road.

Leeds, 22 September 1949
Leeds tram No. 473 fell into a pit at the Leeds Swinegate Depot on 22 September 1949. The car formerly belonged to Hull Tramways. (*Photograph from John Law Collection*)

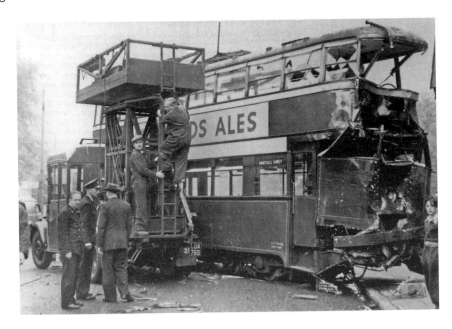

Leeds, 4 September 1952

Leeds sales manager James Penwarden scrambled over the unconscious driver of a tram to bring it to a standstill on Thursday evening 4 September 1952. It was careering out of control at 40-50 mph after being struck by another runaway tram that had travelled nearly a mile without crew or passengers. The accident occurred at Oakwood, Leeds, during the rush hour. Fifteen people were injured. The driverless tram was waiting at Roundhay Park to start its journey back to Kirkstall Abbey. Suddenly, it started to move with only the conductor Percy Cunningham on board. It gathered speed down the incline towards the start of the express track, and about 300 yards from Roundhay Park, Cunningham fell off on to the track. At Oakwood, a Headingley-bound tram had just finished picking up passengers and was beginning to move off when the runaway tram crashed into the back of it, completely wrecking the conductor's platform and staircase. The front tram shot forward and ran nearly a quarter of a mile before it was brought under control. The first runaway tram jumped off the rails after the collision, ran on for about 50 yards on the tarmac road, and was stopped by the pavement edge about 10 feet from the shop fronts of Oakwood Parade. The picture on the left is the tram that ran away; on the right, the tram that was hit by the runaway. (*Pictures courtesy of Yorkshire Post Newspapers*)

Liverpool, 22 January 1906

On the morning of 22 January 1906, Liverpool Corporation's double-decker car No. 447 was descending Leece Street, one of the steepest gradients in the city, did not take the corner into Renshaw Street properly, and was overturned. The car was travelling from Smithdown Road, Wavertree, to the city, with a full complement of business men and women. It had seating accommodation for sixty-four passengers, but nine passengers were also standing in the lower compartment. A large number of people were injured in the accident, but only one seriously. A police constable who was on point duty at the time stated that he saw the driver had lost control of the car, but he was powerless to do anything except to sound a warning whistle for other vehicles to keep out of the way. The cause of the accident was put down partly to driver error. A report afterwards also advised some adjustment to a certain section of track.

Paddington, Liverpool, 3 January 1934

Double-deck, top-covered car No. 181 overturned as the result of a runaway down a 1 in 19 gradient at Paddington, Liverpool, on 3 January 1934. The tram derailed at a curve at the foot of the hill and three people died in the incident. Around thirty people were injured.

Abbey Wood, London, 1940

Built in 1910, Abbey Wood Depot (owned by London County Council Tramways), Abbey Wood Road, Greenwich, sustained severe bomb damage during November 1940. The trams seen in the top picture include Nos 1317, 1028, 826, 1371, 1241. In 1952, the building was converted into a bus garage following the withdrawal of London's tram services. The last tram in London ran from New Cross to Abbey Wood (the 72 route) on 5 July 1952. Abbey Wood closed in the 1980s

Right: Caledonian Road, Barnsbury, London

Built in 1909, London County Council Tramways vehicle No. 1268 is pictured after a collision on 25 May 1935 in Caledonian Road, Barnsbury, Islington. The tram was operating on route 17 and was travelling between Farringdon Street Station and Nags Head; the accident occurred on the King's Cross to Holloway stretch of the route. The tram survived until September 1939.

Below: Blackfriars Bridge, London

Tram derailment at the corner of Blackfriars Bridge on 10 July 1918. The view, facing north, is virtually unrecognisable today.

Archway, London, 23 June 1906

On Saturday afternoon 23 June 1906, there was a disaster in Archway Road, Highgate, London, on one of the busiest tram lines under the Middlesex County Council's control. Just after 4 p.m., double-decker car No. 115, belonging to the Metropolitan Electric Tramways Company, got beyond control when opposite the Archway Tavern. Dashing down a steep hill at a rapid pace, it wrecked a

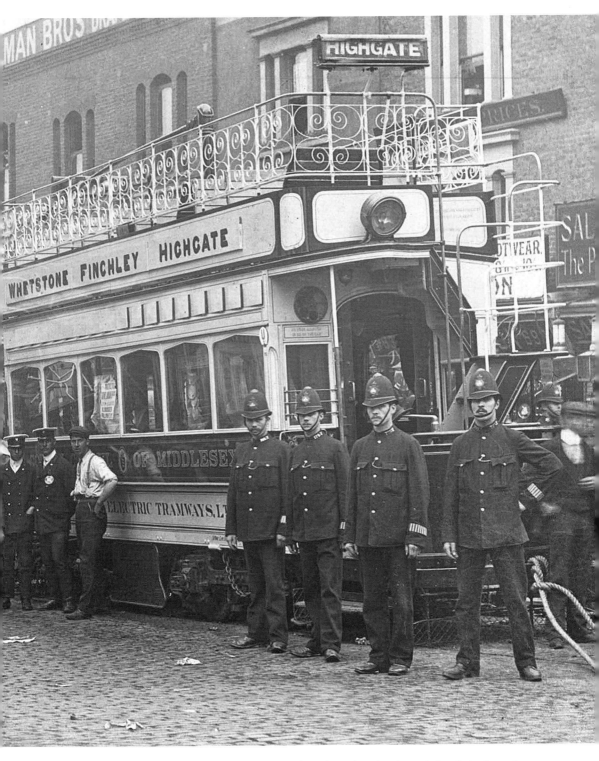

funeral hearse, a van, a Vanguard motorbus, a cab, and another electric car before being brought to a standstill by an electric lamp standard that was in its way. Three people were killed, and approx. twenty injured. A number of passengers, including the driver, jumped from the vehicle during the course of events. The driver received cut and bruises, and accident was put down to his inability to react accordingly to the situation that had presented itself.

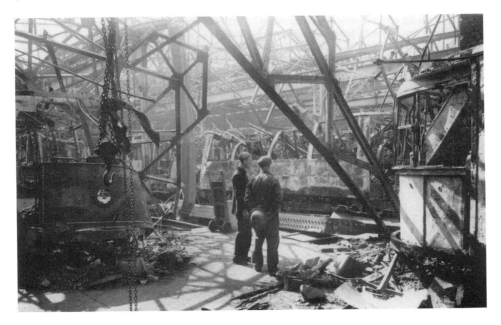

Camberwell Depot, London

View in the Camberwell tram depot on 11 September 1940 where over twenty-five trams were damaged in an air raid that had occurred three days earlier.

Cricklewood, London, 27 June 1916

Shortly before 2.30 p.m. on Tuesday 27 June 1916, a Hendon-Acton car – open-top, double-decker, No. 107 – was travelling in the direction of Cricklewood Corner. When passing Ashford Road, it collided with a heavy War Department motor lorry, which suddenly came round the corner. The impact threw the car off the metals and caused it to overturn, the top part falling across the footway. Fortunately, there were only about a dozen passengers on the car at the time, but they suffered from shock or slight injuries. The most serious injury was sustained by the conductor Frederick J. Williams, who had a fractured left thigh. Simpson, the driver of the lorry, had chest injuries. The badly damaged overturned car remained in Cricklewood Broadway until 11.30 a.m. the next morning and attracted hundreds of sightseers. The motor lorry was only slightly damaged.

Carshalton, London, 1 April 1907

The South Metropolitan Electric Tramways & Lighting Company witnessed an accident on its Croydon-Sutton route around 3.30 p.m. on Bank Holiday Monday 1 April 1907. Immediately after passing over a railway bridge between Wallington and Sutton, cars ran down a hill at Park Lane until they reached the corner of Ruskin road where the line turned sharp round, the latter road being at right angles. Open-top car No. 19, on reaching the sharp corner, took it at such a rapid rate that it overturned. Being holiday time, the tram was crowded with passengers, especially on the top, and they were all shot off into the road. Two people were killed and approx. thirty-four injured. A report concluded that the accident was the result of the driver's inexperience in handling the vehicle, interference by the conductor in applying the handbrake, and overcrowding, especially on the top deck.

Chatham, London

On Friday morning 31 October 1902, four men were killed and approx. fifty were injured in a tram accident at Chatham. Car No. 19 belonging to the Chatham & District Light Railways Company started at about 6.30 a.m. from what was known as Jezreelite Temple, loaded with approx. sixty-five workmen, mainly dockers. The tram was built to accommodate less than were standing on both the bottom and top decks. The tram route was down Westcourt Street, Old Brompton, which was a steep incline, and at the bottom of the hill there was a sharp turn. It was at this spot that the car left the rails and overturned. A number of men, realising an accident was imminent, jumped from the top of the car. Driver Pearce stuck to his post and escaped without serious injury, as did the conductor. The accident was put down to a number of factors, not least the overcrowding, the inexperience of the driver, and the absence of one of the 'pilots' – men employed by the company to travel with a car down the steep hill.

Chatham, London

A Chatham & District Light Railways car, working the Victoria Bridge-Chatham Cemetery service, ran out of control on 15 July 1908 and struck a dockyard wall. Fortunately, the accident only caused minor injuries to the driver and conductor.

Clapham, London, April 1941

View of Clapham tram depot after it was hit by an aerial bombardment on 16 April 1941. The incident caused the loss of two trams. An earlier strike on 15 September 1940 resulted in the loss of eleven cars.

Above: **Embankment, London, 11 September 1951**
On 11 September 1951, a double-decker London bus collided with a double-decker, covered-top tram. The incident occurred on the Embankment, near Temple Underground Station, and the bus, as can be seen here in the view facing west, overturned. Thirteen people were injured, and two of these were seriously hurt.

Opposite: **Kennington, London, September 1940**
Two views of car No. 1385, badly damaged as a result of an air raid in Kennington, during September 1940.

Lewisham, London, 2 September 1911

One person was killed and thirty-five injured when London County Council Tramway's double-decker car No. 110 rounded a bend extending from Shardeloes Road into Lewsham High Road during the afternoon of 2 September 1911 and tipped over. The cause of the accident was largely put down to the learner driver at the controls of the tram not being properly supervised by an experienced driver alongside him.

New Cross Depot, London

The scene at New Cross Depot on 28 December 1940, showing bomb damage. The aerial bombardment had taken place on 21 December and caused the loss of three trams. Car No. 972, built in 1907, seen on the left in the bottom picture, was destroyed, and went for scrap in January 1941.

Above left: **St George's Circus, London, 30 April 1937**
A view taken at St George's Circus on 30 April 1937 after a collision involving car No. 1596, and
E3170.

Above right: **Westminster, London 24 April 1940**
Car No. 1903 was involved in a collision with a lorry on 24 April 1940. Only a few months later,
the vehicle was completely destroyed in the Camberwell Depot air raid.

Woolwich, London, 18 April 1946

People sleeping nearly a quarter-of-a-mile away were awakened early on Thursday morning 18 April 1946 when a runaway 72 workman's tram, LPTB third series E/1 class No. 576, crashed broadside into a shop on Woolwich New Road. The tram got out of control negotiating the steep Grand Depot Road and left the track near the junction of Woolwich New Road and Anglesea Hill. Crossing the up line, it ran almost parallel with the track for a few yards, and then mounted the pavement, coming to rest against the front of the RACS pharmacy store, leaning towards the road at an angle of 80 degrees. Passenger were thrown from their seats to the floor as the tram lurched across the pavement. Four passengers were taken to St Nicholas Hospital, Plumpstead, for treatment. Slight injuries were sustained by the tram driver E. M. Thorburn and the conductor A. C. Weston. The car was severely damaged, and was towed away by breakdown tender. The front of the RACS pharmacy was completely wrecked, and the shops on either side were damaged. A. W. Crosbie, wholesale tobacconist who lived next door, had just got out of bed when the crash occurred. He heard screams and the whole building shook, and then the ceiling fell on top of him. He narrowly escaped serious injury. The rooms above the RACS premises were fortunately unoccupied. After the tram had been towed away, workmen shored up the premises.

Luton, 27 December 1916

A derailment occurred on the Luton Corporation Tramways system around 11.30 a.m. on 27 December 1916. It took place at the junction of Midland Road and Old Bedford Road. Before the junction there was a steep incline that ended in a curve that was little more than a right angle. This demanded the greatest care in negotiation, as more than one car had left the track. On 27 December, the car in question was travelling down High Town Road with seven or eight passengers on board, and nearing the bend, gathered tremendous speed. Failing to negotiate the curve, it overran the rails, swept over the kerbstone, struck an electric standard, and finally crashed through the wooden fence into the earth bank abutting the Midland Railway bridge. The tram was badly damaged, and the motorman Alfred Lloyd was seriously injured. The conductor Arthur Eaton suffered shock, and a number of the passengers were hurt, including the acting chief constable W. J. Hagley who was travelling on the tram.

St Annes, Lytham, 1 April 1907

The *Lytham Times* of Friday 5 April 1907 reported that Lytham had 'a Bank Holiday sensation' when a collision took place about 9.30 a.m. on the morning of Easter Monday, 1 April 1907. Lytham open-top, double-decker car No. 18 (travelling east along Clifton Street towards Lytham Cottage Hospital) collided with a three-horsed picnic caravan that was crossing south-north on Station Road on its way to Singelton. There were no serious casualties, but the newspaper said, 'The inside equipment of the van suffered considerably, and the road flowed with milk whilst dressed chickens were thrown here and there. The horses fortunately kept their heads although they trembled with fear.'

The Car Smash At New Ferry

ELECTRIC CAR SMASH IN THE FOG. AT NEW FERRY.

New Ferry, 23 October 1913

The *Birkenhead News* of 25 October 1913 said the dense fog that enveloped the whole of Merseyside on Thursday morning 23 October was responsible for a tram crash at New Ferry. Fortunately, only one person, the driver of one of the cars Henry Wainwright, was severely injured, although several others were badly shaken and received minor cuts from the flying glass of broken windows. The two cars, which were full of passengers, were travelling in opposite directions; car No. 11, driven by Wainwright, going towards New Ferry having journeyed from Woodside, and No. 64, driven by Elias Torr, having just left the New Ferry terminus on route for Woodside. There was a single track between Rock Lane and the terminus, with loops at intervals, and car No. 11 having entered the loop a few hundred yards from the terminus, waited for a short time for No. 64 to pass. The fog was dense, and thinking that the driver of No. 64 must be waiting for him, resumed his journey. Suddenly however, the glare of the lamp of the approaching car loomed through the fog, and before he had time to apply his brake, the cars had dashed into each other. The fronts of both cars were badly damaged. The dashboard of car No. 11 car was completely carried away, and most of the forward portion of the car was smashed, including the supports, which were wrenched out of position and twisted. When the collision occurred, Wainwright was flung against the body of the car and then on to the roadway. The other driver Elias Torr was more fortunate, escaping with cuts on the scalp and suffering from shock. The work of removing the cars was organised by Cyril Clark, the tramways manager, who was early on the scene of the accident. In foggy weather where the collision occurred, a signal was in use, and was turned on at the depot. It exhibited a light directly opposite the loop, and it was thought the fog must have concealed this signal from the view of Wainwright, who supposing that the line was then clear, proceeded on his way to New Ferry.

Newcastle, 18 October 1913
At Benton, near Newcastle, on Saturday morning 18 October 1913, two trams – double-decker
car No. 23 and trolley wagon No. 27 – collided head-to-head in thick fog. Two of the Tyneside
Tramways & Tramroads Company's staff – including one of the drivers W. Amis – were killed, and
six people injured.

Newcastle, 26 June 1924
Double-decker car No. 251, belonging to Newcastle Corporation Tramways, dashed into a house
in Stanhope Street on 26 June 1924. No serious casualties were recorded.

Pontypridd, 3 May 1919

In the early hours of Saturday morning 3 May 1919, open-top, double-decker car No. 7, returning from Cilfinydd to the tramway depot, got out of control while descending Corn Stores Hill, Pontypridd. The driver Stanley Edwards, together with the conductress and inspector Miss Airons (who were the only occupants of the car), stuck to their posts. Despite the number of sharp turnings on the route, the car kept to the rails travelling at a great speed until it reached the awkward turn into Taff Street. It failed to negotiate that curve, left the rails, and crashed right into the lock-up shop of Messr W. M. Harris & Co., grocers, 38 Taff Street. Miss Airons sustained slight injuries to the knee, but the other two occupants of the car escaped injury. It was fortunate that the streets were deserted when the accident occurred at 6.15 a.m.

Opposite: **Pontypridd, 22 March 1920**
On 22 March 1920, Pontypridd double-decker car No. 66 got out of control, largely due to the slippery condition of the rails and there being no sand, only crushed clinker available on the vehicle. The car was in the charge of an experienced driver and was practically full of passengers. After starting on a down gradient, the brakes failed to act. The street at this time was congested with pedestrians and vehicles, and when near the bend of the road, the car collided with a lorry. Gaining speed, the car dashed over the river bridge where it struck a delivery cart. At the entrance to Mill Street, a milk cart was caught broadside on. But when the runaway car took a turn into Market Street, it failed to cross a set of points and tumbled over on to its right side. The most extraordinary part of the affair was that all the passengers in the tram escaped serious injury. The driver stuck bravely to his car the whole distance.

Above: **Queensbury, 3 December 1920**
Heavy rainstorms, accompanied by a fierce wind that blew in violent gusts, occurred on Friday 3 December 1920 over a great part of the north of England, the Midlands, and off the coasts. Three people were very fortunate to escape with only slight injuries in a tramway accident on the Halifax system. During Friday afternoon, two double-decker cars Nos 98 and 50 were blown over on the exposed Queensbury route at Catherine Slack. The first car, which contained only three people, was hurled over at a point nearly 1,000 feet above sea level, and the second car, which was empty, met a similar fate almost at the same place, two or three hours later.

Ramsgate, 26 May 1905

On Friday 26 May 1905, loop-line car No. 47, with driver David O'Connor and conductor William Hyde, was involved in a mishap. After the customary stop at Thanet Road, the car gathered speed, and failing to turn a corner, left the rails and dashed into the grocery stores of Messrs Vye & Son. The shop was badly damaged, and the car partly embedded within the premises. Approx. seven people were injured, but not seriously. Fortunately, the car was only carrying four passengers. Driver O'Connor leapt from the car when it jumped the rails. Within the shop were William Leno, the manager, and his niece Edith Gregory. The manager escaped injury, but the little girl was crushed amid the debris, but recovered.

Ramsgate, 3 August 1905

Just before noon on 3 August 1905, Isle of Thanet open-top, double-decker car No. 41, containing several passengers, left the rails on the East Cliff at Ramsgate, and toppled over the cliff a distance of approx. 30 feet. In the car were five passengers and the conductor, and all were thrown to the bottom with the vehicle. The driver was hurled on to a disused building and sustained severe injuries. The car was badly damaged, but the injuries to the passengers and conductor were slight. The Thanet trams ran over a route full of difficult slopes and awkward curves, and had the car left the rails some forty yards lower down, the passengers might have been thrown into the water of the inner harbour.

Ramsgate, 3 August 1905

A visitor to the town said he saw the Ramsgate car suddenly swerve off the line at right angles, crash into the fence, hang temporarily on to the wall, then drop over the cliff. He could see the passengers holding on to the straps as the car overturned. When it reached the bottom, the undercarriage came away from the woodwork and lay in a twisted mass. The inexperience of the driver, in his ability to control the car's braking system, was partly to blame for the accident. The top picture gives some idea of the distance that the tram fell; the one below, the location where the car left the track.

Scene of Tram accident   Ramsgate   3rd Aug 05
Showing where Car went over Cliff.

Rochdale, 14 February 1914

On Saturday night 14 February 1914, Rochdale Corporation Tramways system experienced a mishap. Running from Whitworth, single-decker car No. 63 was travelling down John Street – a 1 in 16 gradient – when it began to skid. The driver Harry Sansom applied the brakes, but they failed to stop the car, which raced down the hill at high speed, and half way down the lights went out. On reaching the bend into Smith Street, the car jumped the metals, raced across the road, collided with a tramway standard, and then ran into the Rochdale Pioneers' butcher's shop. The driver, who never left his post until the impact took place, was badly injured. A number of passengers were also seriously hurt.

Opposite: Scarborough, 10 September 1923

On Wednesday 10 September 1923, double-decked Scarborough tram No. 21 ran backwards down Vernon Place in the town – which has a gradient of one in nine – crashed through a stone wall bordering the top of the Aquarium, and plunged through the glass roof of the building falling end-on in the ballroom 30 feet below. The amazing part of the extraordinary accident is that no one was killed, and only three persons were slightly injured – the driver of the car George Darley Smith – who courageously stuck to his post and was found among the wreckage – and two visitors from Pudsey, Police Constable Robinson and his wife.

Above: Scarborough

By tram, the journey up the Vernon Place hill was always a slow one, and after travelling upwards for about 120 yards, car No. 21 stopped – and then began to glide backwards down the incline. Mr and Mrs Robinson, noting that the driver's desperate efforts to check the car were in vain, became alarmed, and they hurried to the platform and jumped off, falling into the roadway. It was not far to the curve of the line at the Aquarium top, but the car had by then gained sufficient momentum to prevent it remaining on the lines at the bend. With the driver still at his post strenuously trying to make the brake act, the car left the metals at the curve, spun across the narrow margin between the tract and the Aquarium, and plunged into the ballroom. People standing in the area were for the moment paralysed, and no one expected that driver Smith would be found alive. But a few minutes later, he was found among the wreckage of the tram, wedged down by a seat. He had been thrown from his end of the car to the other. He was dazed, and bleeding from a wound to his forehead, and after being attended by a nurse and ambulance men was taken to hospital. PC Robinson escaped with abrasions and severe shock. Mrs Robinson sustained a broken ankle and was suffering from shock. The conductor A. Wike dropped off the car at the bend and escaped injury, but he was also affected by shock. The cause of the accident was attributed to the tram losing its grip on a problematic section of track near the top of the incline.

Sheffield, 27 March 1902

Sheffield Corporation single-deck car no. 156 was standing at the Intake terminus on Thursday afternoon 27 March 1902, when the conductor, thinking he had heard the bell (to move off), took off the brake. The driver was not in his place and the car ran down a hill, on one of the steepest routes on the system, towards the city. The passengers were terrified, but powerless, and before the conductor could pull up the car, it left the rails and crashed into a wall. Fortunately, only two of the passengers sustained injuries and they were not serious. Both the driver and the conductor, deemed to have acted negligently, were subsequently dismissed.

Sheffield Blitz, December 1940

Sheffield was the target for German bombers on Thursday 12 December and Sunday 15 December 1940. The first attack caused disruption to the tramway system and bombs were dropped in many areas of the city. In total, fourteen cars were destroyed and others needed repairs. For a time, this put tramway services under severe pressure, especially at busy times.

Sheffield Blitz, December 1940
Wrecked and burning cars in High Street, Sheffield, following the air raid of December 1940.

Sheffield, 17 July 1950

Sheffield Corporation double-decker car No. 438, travelling to Sheffield Lane Top, was in collision with a runaway lorry in Derbyshire Lane on 17 July 1950. The tram overturned and was damaged beyond repair. The last of the original trams in Sheffield ran between Leopold Street to Beauchief and Tinsley on 8 October 1960.

Sowerby Bridge, 15 October 1907

An accident took place on the morning of Tuesday 15 October 1907 on the steep hill known as Pye Nest, Sowerby Bridge, resulting in the death of five people and injuring approx. thirty-seven. Halifax Corporation car No. 64 left Sowerby Bridge at about 5.30 a.m. crammed with working people who had to be at the mills at Halifax at 6.00 a.m. All appeared to have gone well until Pye Nest Park was reached, when the car began to back down the hill. Driver T. Simpson applied the brake, but his efforts were in vain. The car gathered speed, and when the junction of Bolton Brow was reached, it left the rails, ran into a shop, and overturned.

Sowerby Bridge, 15 October 1907

The conductor T. Robinson was pinned under the car, and was found to be dead when freed. A large number of local doctors and ambulance men quickly appeared on the scene, and had the injured removed into neighbouring houses and the Shepherd's Rest Hotel. The shop into which the car crashed belonged to Lewis Atkinson, grocer and draper, who stated he was in bed at the time of the incident. The cause of the accident was said to be partly the result of a break in the power supply.

CAR ACCIDENT
MILLBROOK
STALYBRIDGE
APRIL 2.190

Stalybridge, 2 April 1908

On 2 April 1908, Stalybridge, Hyde, Mossley & Dukinfield Tramways & Electricity Board's car No. 25 got out of control while descending a steep hill at Mill Brook, and on reaching a sudden turn at the bottom, it jumped the metals. It ran along the road for about 30 yards, turned suddenly to the right, and only just missed running into a public house by a foot. The car crashed into some

railings that ran alongside a brook and plunged bodily into the stream. The driver was dashed among some stones in the brook, receiving a gash to his face and bruises to his body. The conductor was not seriously hurt, and the only passenger escaped injury by jumping off the car. Thousands of people, attracted by the novel spectacle of a tram car in a brook, subsequently visited the scene of the accident.

Stalybridge, 5 June 1911

Double-decker car No. 44, belonging to the Stalybridge, Hyde, Mossley & Dukinfield Tramways & Electricity Board, left Stalybridge for Hadens, near Mossley, at 5.45 a.m. on 5 June 1911, and it was carrying a large number of people on their way to work. At the top of Ditchcroft Hill, it was claimed in contemporary newspaper reports, that the trolley came off the overhead wires and then the car rushed down the hill. The vehicle kept to the metals until about three-quarters of the way down when a sharp curve had to be negotiated. Here the car left the rails and careered across the road, finally overturning opposite the Sportsman Inn at the foot of the hill. Driver John Napper tried in vain to check the car, and when it overturned, was flung from the platform, suffering injuries. One person was killed and a large number hurt. Fortunately, the local cotton mills were not working on that day; if they had been, the car might have been carrying around ninety passengers.

Sunderland, 1 April 1916
Car No. 10, belonging to Sunderland & District Tramways, was wrecked by a bomb dropped from a German Zeppelin airship on Saturday 1 April 1916. The explosion also killed an inspector.

Sunderland, September 1921
In September 1921, Sunderland & District Tramways double-decker car No. 33 ran out of control and tipped over in Brompton Terrace, Newbottle. The accident occurred not far from the tram depot.

Opposite above: Sunderland, 15 June 1933

Around 3 p.m. on Thursday afternoon 15 June 1933, thirteen people were injured when Sunderland Corporation Tramways double-decker car No. 70 overturned as a result of a collision in Hylton Road with a brewer's lorry. All the injured were taken to Sunderland Royal Infirmary and treated for bruises, cuts, and shock. They were all allowed to go home after treatment. The accident occurred as the tram was travelling west, just after leaving Millfield Station. The brewer's lorry had turned out of a side street, and the tram had reached the bottom of the short hill when they collided. Fortunately, there was little other traffic and few people about at the time the tram turned over on to its side. The driver of the tram T. Hall was uninjured, but suffered shock. The conductor said that could not remember much about the accident, but also suffered shock.

Opposite below: Sunderland, 3 January 1952

After packed Sunderland car No. 96 was involved in an accident with a double-deck bus outside the Sunderland Royal Infirmary on 3 January 1952, it left the track, crashed into a tram standard, and came to rest almost broadside on against Burn Park railings. An eye witness said, 'There is no doubt it would have crashed down the 35 feet drop into the park if the course had not been broken by the tram standard.' The tram driver Samuel Topliss was treated at the infirmary for injuries to his right hand. Seven of the passengers were also treated at the hospital. (*Photograph courtesy of Sunderland Echo*)

Above: Swindon, 1 June 1906

On Friday evening 1 June 1906, Swindon Corporation trams were heavily laden with passengers travelling to and from the Bath and West of England Agricultural Show. Open top car No. 11, which was registered to carry fifty-eight passengers with seven standing downstairs, was descending Victoria Road – a steep incline connecting the old and new parts of Swindon – with a load of approx. eighty people. Midway down the hill, the car lost control, and at the bottom, ran on to the up rails at a crossing and overturned. A small number of passengers jumped clear, but five people were killed and a large number injured. The main cause of the accident was attributed to poor maintenance of the car's braking system and a lack of communication between tramway staff.

Swinton, 30 July 1908

One of the steepest gradients on the tramway system connecting Rotherham with Mexborough, South Yorkshire, was at Warren Hill, Swinton (between Rawmarsh and Kilnhurst). On Thursday morning 30 July 1908, the Mexborough & Swinton Tramways Company car No. 14, filled with colliers on their way to work, went out of control due to a brake failure on the (1 in 10) hill and gathered speed. On entering a loop, the points were safely negotiated, but on leaving it, the car left the metals, swerved to the right and then to the left, demolishing a wall, and dropped in to a garden 10 feet below the road. The driver and inspector both stuck to their posts and escaped with a shaking. Although alarmed, the passengers escaped without serious injury, with the exception of one man, who jumped from the car and sustained a broken collar bone. Others were bruised and cut by broken glass. The manager and a staff of men were speedily at the scene, and those who required medical aid were sent to the parish doctors. In every case, the men could walk home.

Swinton, 30 July 1908

Driver Ferguson, on finding that the car was out of control and that he could not check the pace, allowed the inspector to take charge, but he also was powerless. The system as originally laid down was one using surface contact. But owing to electrical difficulties in working, this was being substituted by overhead power collection. The transition had been accomplished to within half a mile of the accident.

Wallasey, 19 March 1907

On 19 March, 1907, a Wallasey Corporation double-decker car ran out of control in Seabank Road before leaving the track and finishing on the pavement alongside a garden wall. Thankfully, there were no casualties.

Warwick, 3 January 1916

On 3 January 1916, Leamington & Warwick Electrical Company Ltd's open-top, double-decker car No. 7 crashed into the Castle Arms Inn, Warwick. The accident was put down to human error – the driver forgot to leave the handbrake on. Three people sustained injuries.

CHAPTER 2

Foreign Crashes and Accidents

AUSTRALIA

Melbourne, Australia, 20 March 1968
'I dived for the brake when a red sports car swerved in front of the tram – then somehow I hit my head on the glass window and everything went black.' This is what tram driver John Middlemo said on 20 March 1968 after a spectacular two-tram collision at the corner of Flinders Street and Swanston Street, Melbourne, Victoria, Australia. His tram was travelling west towards Spencer St, and the Swanston St tram was travelling north. John was one of thirty-one people taken to hospital after the pile up. No one was seriously hurt, but thousands of people jamming the intersection after the accident made it difficult for the eight ambulances. A small late-model sedan, driven by Mrs G. Thompson was grazed by the Swanston St tram when it was forced off the rails. The conductor of the Flinders St tram, Carl Barrett said: 'I was thrown to the floor when we hit the other tram and money and broken glass flew everywhere. A woman fell on top of me and started screaming and I could see another woman nearby was bleeding from a gash in her arm.' (*Photograph © Newspix / Ian Brown*)

Brisbane, 23 April 1949
An accident involving a tram and bus (travelling to the Valley) in Brisbane on 23
April 1949. Two men are inspecting the damage while a group of bus and/or tram
conductors look on, seemingly laughing. (*Photograph courtesy of the State Library of
Queensland, Australi*a)

Brisbane, 4 June 1935
Motor vehicle squashed between two early electric trams in McLachlan Street,
Brisbane, Australia, on 4 June 1935. (*Photograph courtesy of the State Library of
Queensland, Australia*)

Mascot, pre-1955
Tram pictured after a collision in Botany Road, Mascot, Sydney, Australia, during the 1950s.

Collision between tram and coal truck on Botany Road, Mascot, during the early 1940s.

Left: Melbourne, 1922

A Point Ormonde tram after an accident in 1922, pictured in a tram shed awaiting repair. The car's indicator box has been damaged in the accident and is only showing 'Ormond'. The Point Ormond route was a very short shuttle that ran to and from Elstnerwick Station and was the first postwar tram abandonment in Melbourne, latterly being operated by an imported Birney tram.

Below: Miranda, 1924

On Tuesday 11 November 1924, Australian newspaper *The Mercury* reported that one man was killed and twelve people were slightly injured when a steam tram travelling from Sutherland to Cronulla had run off the line at Miranda early that morning. The engine plunged down an embankment and turned over, crushing the driver, and one of the two cars also ran down the bank, but it remained on its wheels. The two cars of the tram were filled with passengers and they all suffered from shock, but none was seriously hurt. The man who was killed, Samuel Weche, was the driver of the engine. The steam tram was on the South Coast railway to the beach towns. Weche had been in the tramway service for thirty years, but had been driving the steam tram for only a few months.

Sydney, 25 June 1937

On 25 June 1937, a taxi pulled out from the curb on Pitt Street, Sydney, and collided with one of the city's 'toast rack' trams. The coupling of the tram penetrated the right side of the cab.

CANADA

Toronto *c.* 1935

A truck and streetcar were involved in an accident on Danforth Avenue, Toronto, *c.* 1935. (*Photographer: William James*)

GERMANY

Munich, 17 December 1960

On 17 December 1960, an American transport aircraft bound for Northolt crashed on a tram in the centre of Munich. About fifty people were killed, including everyone in the aircraft. The plane struck a church spire four minutes after taking off from Munich airport, and then it fell on the rear half of a three-compartment tram. Fire broke out immediately from a gas main broken by the impact and from the aircraft's fuel. Herr Vogel, the Mayor of Munich, who took charge of the rescue operations, announced a week of mourning in the city. It was stated that the pilot appeared to have lost direction in fog. He radioed that he was in trouble and tried to land on a fairground site.

HOLLAND

Overtoom, Amsterdam, 1936

The truck was trying to make a right hand turn into the Jan Pieter Heijestraat and collided with a tram from route 6. The bowcollector had already been turned to facilitate the tram to turn back. Trams (and all other traffic) had right of way over turning traffic. It has been said that Amsterdam tram drivers had a reputation of exercising their right of way any which way!

Amsterdam, April 1946

British Army truck – Fordson type WOT6 – three-tonner – competes with tram No. 312 in Amsterdam during April 1946. (*Photograph by Ben van Meerendonk / AHF, collection International Institute of Social History, Amsterdam, Holland*)

Amsterdam, 6 April 1956

Tom Mulder was a passenger on two-axle tram No. 453 at the time of the crash in Frederik Hendrikplantsoen/Nassaukade and said the following: 'On April 6 1956, I caught tram 453 on line three on the Haarlemmerplein to visit my grandparents. As usual I went to my favourite spot in the front compartment of the tram on the left hand side of the driver. I recognized the driver, not so long ago he was still a conductor. His peaked cap still displayed the star, the cap symbol for conductors. Drivers of trams would sport wings on their caps which may be considered symbolic of the driving style of some of the drivers. The driver was relatively young, about thirty, and he drove faster than necessary or indeed safe in the narrow streets from the Haarlemmerplein to the Marnixplein, which, by the way, I quite enjoyed. When we reached the Marnixplein we had to negotiate a switch separating the route of line 3 and 10. From the right, a big truck and trailer on the Nassaukade was also approaching the Marnixplein intersection. The tram driver saw the truck coming, in the distance and braked defensively, anticipating he just could go ahead without losing momentum after the truck had passed the intersection. However the tram driver misjudged the situation and crashed into the trailer of the truck. I saw it all happening of course. The front section of the tram was ripped off, the driver was smashed on to the street. I had made two steps backwards when the truck was reaching the 453 and was staring at the void that once was the front of the tram. The controller was lying on the road. I stayed on the tram until the ambulance officers got me. Both the tram driver and me were taken to the hospital. There were no other casualties. The driver sustained relatively minor injuries breaking two bones in his foot. I was treated for minor cuts and shock and discharged when my parents collected me.' (*Photograph by Ben van Meerendonk / AHF, collection International Institute of Social History, Amsterdam*)

Amsterdam, February 1950
A Budapester tram, on the narrow gauge railway from Amsterdam to Haarlem Spui, is derailed at
the Admiraal de Ruyterweg, February 1950. (*Photograph by Ben van Meerendonk / AHF, collection
International Institute of Social History, Amsterdam*)

Amsterdam, 6 September 1950
Tram No. 263 derailed on the intersection with the tracks of line 9 on 6 September 1950, and pushed a parked car through a railing into the Amstel. The tram landed on top of the motorcar, preventing it from falling further into the water. There were no casualties. The Amstel is only about 2 metres deep near the water's edge. The tram driver walked away with wet trousers (below the knees) only. (*Photograph by Ben van Meerendonk / AHF, collection International Institute of Social History, Amsterdam*)

Opposite above: Amsterdam, 14 April 1947
A truck of the Dutch Railways has collided with a tram on 14 April 1947. (*Photograph by Ben van Meerendonk / AHF, collection International Institute of Social History, Amsterdam*)

Opposite below: Amsterdam, 21 October 1951
Tram 10 collides with a Vami milk truck on the Mauritskade, Amsterdam, 21 October 1951. (*Photograph by Ben van Meerendonk / AHF, collection International Institute of Social History, Amsterdam*)

Amsterdam, 7 October 1969

Trams 615 and 619 collide head-on at the Crossing Woustraat and Ceintuurbaan. This photo was taken on 7 October 1969 by Henk Graalman, who said: 'The accident happened because the driver of the 615 had not noticed the hand-operated switches/points showing left turn. The hand operated switches/points were mainly used during diversions and not part of service routes where all switches were electric. After crossing hand-operated switches the conductors used to put it back after the tram had passed. When conductors were phased out this was no longer the case resulting in some serious frontal collisions as drivers had been in a comfort zone only paying attention to electric switches.'

Amsterdam, 11 January 1950

The tram driver was killed in this collision with a Chevrolet C6oL lorry on tramline 10 at the Zeeburgerdijk corner Celebesstraat and Borneostraat, Amsterdam, on 11 January 1950. According to the newspaper *Het Parool*, the tram allegedly may have had a brake malfunction and hit the stationary truck. Former Dutch resident and photogrpaher Henk Graalman said the following: 'Line 3 and 10 have historically and proportionally recorded most of the serious and spectacular tram crashes in Amsterdam. There are some reasons for this. Both tramroutes cross the busy ring road Zeeburgerdijk/Mauritskade/Stadshouderskade/Nassaukade. These connecting roads are wide and well laid out and served as the main entry road as well as the ring road for the city of Amsterdam, and as such carry a lot of heavy traffic. Over time trucks were hauling heavier loads, got bigger and started to tow trailers, particularly after the second world war in 1945. And, admittedly generalizing, some truckdrivers regularly would cut off or cut in front of trams, not realizing or ignorant of the fact that the tram had right of way as well as that the emergency braking ability of old trams was non existent. The privilege of right of way of trams in Amsterdam was warmly embraced, used and abused by some tram drivers. And a tram driver could only apply the electric brake with his controller and had to use the handbrake to come to a full stop, which was adequate for day to day operations but inadequate in the event of an emergency. It is for this reason that rail brakes (blokken) were retro fitted to old twin axle trams in the fifties and sixties. Triple-axle trams delivered 1949 onwards were the first rolling stock factory fitted with railbrakes.' (*Photograph by Ben van Meerendonk / AHF, collection International Institute of Social History, Amsterdam*)

Left: **Amsterdam, 12 August 1970**
Early morning on 12 August 1970, bus 423 en route to the depot had a full frontal collision with tram 683 on route 13, Burgemeester de Vlugtlaan. Both drivers were injured, the bus driver quite seriously. Both recovered well and eventually resumed duties. (*Photograph taken by Henk Graalman*)

Below: **Amsterdam, 9 April 1971**
Henk Graalman photographed this accident involving a Renault 16 and a tram in Amsterdam on 9 April 1971.

Amsterdam, 9 July 1971

A derailment involving No. 559 in the Leidsestraat has brought out technical assistance to sort out the problem on 9 July 1971. (*Photograph by Henk Graalman*)

Osdorp, March 1973

Tram No. 709 collided head-on with a car in Osdorp during March 1973. (*Photograph by Henk Graalman*)

Amsterdam, 22 July 1973

Henk Graalman took this picture on 22 July 1973 in Osdorp, Amsterdam, and said, 'Tramcar 723 derailed after taking a sharp corner a bit fast. Getting the tram back on the rails was a very late night, early morning effort. [Also] the overhead wires had to be fixed and a catenary pole had to be replaced.'

Holland, 29 July 1973

Photograph reproduced courtesy of Henk Graalman, who commented, 'Renault crunched by tram 675 and the 672 moving closer than necessary blocking the intersection PH Kade, on 29 July 1973.'

Amsterdam, 15 September 2000

Photographer Renee Van Lier recorded this incident in Cornelis Lelylaan/stop Piet Wiedijkstraat on 15 September 2000, and related, 'The driver of the empty 834 was distracted and didn't notice that the 817 was standing still at a tramstop and crashed full speed into this tram.'

Amsterdam, October 2001

This photograph dated October 2001 is from Flickr user RoryTait's (Anthony) photostream, and he comments, 'Aftermath of a traffic accident in Amsterdam. Notice FOUR modes of transportation in this photo: bike, car, bus and streetcar!'

NEW ZEALAND

Wellington, Brooklyn, 3 May 1907

On Friday evening 3 May 1907, an accident on the Brooklyn tramway section, Wellington, resulted in the death of one person, and severe injuries to other passengers, the motorman and the conductor. The car left the rails and plunged down an embankment. As may be seen from the photograph, many people visited the scene of the crash.

RUSSIA

Smolensk, 1910
People pose alongside a tram damaged in a collision in Smolensk during 1910.

SWITZERLAND

Lausanne, Switzerland, 27 October 1913
Around midnight on 27 October 1913, there was an accident in Rue du Valentin 25 1004 Lausanne, Switzerland. Whilst travelling too fast taking a curve, the tram crossed the gate of a courtyard, breaking part of the wall and finally crashed against a house, as the picture shows. Two people were killed in the accident, although because it was late, not many people were in the tram, or the number of casualties could have been higher.

Carouge, Genève, Switzerland, 10 April 1932
Tram No. 165 lying at the bottom of the road Drize Roundel Carouge on 10 April 1932. (*Photograph courtesy of Trams to the Son*)

Genève, 1 December 1949
Collision between tram and truck in the Rue du Mont-Blanc on 1 December 1949. (*Photograph courtesy of C.G.T.E. Collection*)

United States

Above and below: **Washington, 1921**
Accident involving car No. 112 in Washington, 1921.

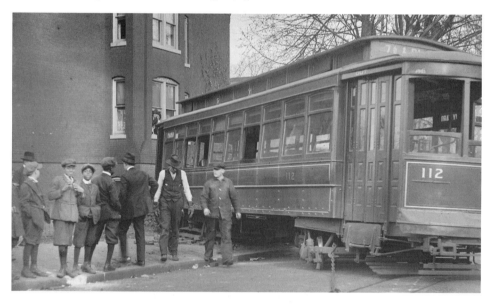

Opposite above: **Adelaide, 10 March 2006**
Bombardier Flexity classic 103 never made it one piece to Adelaide. The story is that the carrying
ship was hit by a freak wave near Cape of Good Hope, causing a serious list, which in turn caused
other cargo to break loose from the lashings and crash into the Metro Adelaide tram 103. It might
be the only tram ever meeting such an unfortunate destiny not earning anything in revenue service.
Replacement car 112 entered service as 103 again. (*Photograph courtesy of Henk Graalman,
bombardier workshop in Melbourne, 10 March 2006*)

CHAPTER 3

British and Foreign Tram Crashes and Accidents in Colour

AUSTRALIA

Below: **Adelaide, 17 June 2009**

Adelaide tram No. 108 and a reversing truck collided in King William Street, Adelaide Central, Adelaide, Australia, at about 7.40 a.m. on 17 June 2009, forcing a closure on some lanes. Henk Graalman, who took the picture, adds: 'The crash happened because the truck intended to reverse 90 degrees into an alley on the right. The truck driver had not paid attention to the tram as he focussed on his mate directing him from the curb. The tram driver had not anticipated the front of the truck swinging back in front of the car. There were no casualties, but the tram driver was treated for shock.'

Melbourne, 22 September 2005
This photograph was taken by Tom R. Keeble on 22 September 2005, and he has related the
following: 'During my walk into the city I bumped into a car which had bumped into a tram.
I didn't think it was that bad, my old granddad did the same thing two decades earlier. I still
remember the purple charger all crushed and pathetic. The car, not the granddad, that is...'

Melbourne, 2 June 2009
Photographer Peggy Kuo was on a short trip to Melbourne to visit friends when she took saw a
tram accident on 2 June 2009 and took a picture of it.

Melbourne, 24 September 2007

Information on Tim and Lucy's Flickr Photostream states: '[The crash] happened on Saint Kilda Road Melbourne on 24 September 2007 around 10 a.m. A number 6 headed northbound to the university went into the back of a No. 72 headed to the same destination. One tram was thrown 2 metres back in the crash, while the other one was derailed. The tram driver of the No. 6 was seriously injured and had to be cut out of the cabin – eleven passengers received minor injuries.' The two trams were the more modern Siemen's Combino low-floor trams, which serviced Melbourne.

New South Wales, Athol Wharf at Mosman, Sydney, 20 July 1952

The 1950s saw three more or less identical runaway tram accidents in this location, where trams heading off down the steep hill to the lower entrance of the famous Taronga Park Zoo in Sydney sped off uncontrollably and ended up in the Athol Wharf at Mosman. The accidents were in 1942, 1952, and 1958. The photograph depicts the recovery effort of the tram in the incident on Sunday Morning 20 July 1952. A newspaper report of 21 July 1952 stated that a runaway tram rushed more than a mile downhill in Bradley's Head Road, Mosman, hurtled 60 feet through the air on to some rocks, and came to rest with its driver's cabin and front seats in the harbour near Taronga Zoo Wharf. Four people were injured – a man and woman, who were the only passengers, and the driver and conductor who jumped clear just before the crash. The tram was the 8.23 a.m. from Balmoral to Athol Wharf. The tide was out and part of the tram landed in water 20 feet deep.

CANADA

Toronto, 18 August 2009
Motor car and tram collision at Queen Quay West, Harbourside, on 18 August 2009. (*Photograph courtesy of Richard Grantham*)

CZECH REPUBLIC

Prague, 15 June 2010
John B. Platt made the following comments about this picture that he took on 15 June 2010: 'Prague's tram route 22 is a great route for the tourist, as it passes the Castle and some stunning views before crossing the city and terminating at Hostiva, also one of the termini of metro route A. As can be seen in this photograph, traffic was able to circumnavigate the obstruction, apart from the trams of course, which began to tail back in a long procession. The accident appeared to have happened a while before we arrived on the scene in a following tram. I didn't see anyone injured or any signs of ambulance. It looked as though the tram was in a fit state to be driven away once the obstruction had been cleared and I think the police were just making measurements and taking photographs before pulling the car clear.'

FINLAND

Helsinki, 13 December, 2011

This photo was taken on 13 December 2011 in Ruoholahti, Helsinki, Southern Finland, by Teemu Ikonen, who stated: 'Power was switched on in the new Saukonpaasi loop on the second week of December 2011. For some reason HKL 2122 derailed when clearing the tracks for traffic (due to commence 1 January 2012). The two axle tram has a long wheelbase which probably contributed to the mishap. I suggest going over the geometry before carrying passengers!'

Helsinki, 23 October 2002

Timo-Pekka took the picture on 23 October 2002 and a local newspaper reported: 'Seven people were injured in Helsinki when two trams collided at the intersection of Mannerheimintie and Runeberginkatu close to the Opera House. The accident took place at 4.10 p.m. in the middle of rush hour traffic. Some of Helsinki's tram routes were out of operation for over two hours, disrupting traffic in downtown Helsinki. The cause of the accident was evidently a malfunction of the switch at the intersection. The end of tram 3B, which was heading south on Mannerheimintie and turning on to Runeberginkatu, evidently missed the switch and continued straight on, lurching in front of an on-coming No. 10 tram. The two trams collided heavily, with seven passengers receiving injuries. Removal of the 3B tram took over two hours, and trams were running off schedule still after 6 p.m.'

FRANCE

Nantes, France, 15 November 2005
Tram and motorcar collision photographed by Flickr user Banlon1964 (Michael O'Connor) on 15 November 2005 in Hauts-Paves-Saint-Felix, Nantes, Pays de la Loire, France.

GREAT BRITAIN

Blackpool, 4 September 2002
Photographer Gary Overend tells in his own words the circumstances surrounding the collision: 'It was growing quite dark when the picture was taken and I initially used a flash but this reflected back from the police car making the image darker so I had to take the photo without a flash resting on my wife's shoulder to try and stop camera shake. The photo was taken on 4 September 2002 at the Pleasure Beach end of Blackpool. The car had tried to exit a car park that crosses over the tramlines to the road, but had failed to spot the approaching tram. The driver of the car can be seen sitting on the steps to the right of the picture.'

Manchester, 1 July 2007
An incident involving a Manchester tram and a Mercedes motor vehicle in Mosley Street, Manchester, on 1 July 2007. (*Photograph courtesy of Ben Clarke – Bensholto's Flickr Photostream*)

Sheffield, 20 February 1997
On 20 February 1997, a bruised vicar called for urgent safety work on Sheffield's Supertram lines after his car overturned at just 20 mph. Rev. Ernest Hume, the vicar of Woodseats, escaped from the wreckage of his Rover with whiplash and bruising. He lost control of the car as he tried to follow a left hand curve. He said: 'I had slowed down because it was [raining heavily] and I knew the lines were slippery. I was trying to straddle the lines with the car, but as the wheels touched the track, the car just shot from under me. It hit the crash barrier and rolled over. I had filled up with petrol and was thinking that if it leaked I could get fried.' Later, Sheffield highways staff investigated the problem of skid resistance on concrete sections of the tram track. (*Photograph courtesy of Rachel Clark*)

Sheffield, 23 March 1999
The scene after a Supertram had collided with a car at the junction of Infirmary Road and Terrace Road Shalesmoor, Sheffield, 10 April 1999. (*Photograph courtesy of Sheffield Newspapers*)

HOLLAND

Amsterdam, April 2002
Lorry and tram collide on a line extending from the central station to the Dam Square, Amsterdam. Nobody was hurt. (*Photographed in April 2002, courtesy of Chico Manobela*)

The Hague, 8 May 2009

Dating from 8 May 2009, this photograph was taken in Leyenburg, the Hague, by Marc Gerritson, who explained, 'The tram was moving from the Leyweg towards the Escamplaan. The bus obviously missed the tram. The tram was just leaving when it happened [...] since the accident a 15 kmph speed limit was introduced for the buses.'

Utrecht, 2 December 2000

'The crane was busy near the Congress-Center of Utrecht and was moving when the tram was just passing with this accident as a result,' said Johan Waaijer who took the picture.

Amsterdam, 27 September 2005
A Landrover collides with a tram in the Linnaeusstraat, Amsterdam, on 27 September 2005. Fortunately, the Landrover driver was unhurt. (*Photograph courtesy of Bas Hiemstra*)

IRELAND

Dublin, 16 September 2009
At 3 p.m. 16 September 2009, there was a collision between a No. 16 Dublin bus AV266, from Ballinteer to Santry in Dublin City Centre, and a Red Line Luas tram 3002 at the junction of Middle Abbey Street and O'Connell Street, Dublin. Twenty-one people were injured as a result of the crash. Three people, including the Luas driver, were cut out of the wreckage. The Luas was derailed in the accident. (*Photograph courtesy of Craig Wade*)

Dublin, 10 September 2012

A tram and a bin truck collided at the junction between Benburb Street and Temple Street, Dublin, on 10 September 2012. Both drivers were taken to hospital as a precautionary measure, but were released a short time afterwards. The tram was derailed and efforts to remove it took several hours. (*Photograph courtesy of Darren Hall*)

ITALY

Trieste, September 2012

Tram 404 was heading back to the Opicina depot when it derailed between the Banne and Obelisco stations. Initially it was suspected that the cause of the derailment was excessive speed, but according to the only passenger on the tram when the accident occurred and to other experts, the vehicle was travelling at a normal speed (it was also travelling uphill). One local said: 'The section of track where the accident happened is in quite bad state, it causes the trams to sway and bang noticeably, in particular after the summer 2012 months, that were very hot. This section of track was renovated in the '70s and '80s using recycled rails from the withdrawn town tram lines.' (*Photograph courtesy of Luchetti Thomas*)

JAPAN

Matsuyama, Japan September 2010
Flickr user Rolfboom says this picture was taken by chance in September 2010 in Matsuyama, Japan.

POLAND

Warsaw, 21 August 2008
Six people were injured, but not seriously, in a tram accident in Warsaw, Poland, at around 8 a.m. on 21 August 2008. (*Photograph courtesy of Wojciech Tylbor-Kubrakiewicz*)

Krakow, 29 May 2007

Photographer Simon Gow was actually on this tram when it crashed, and he describes the incident in his own words: 'I believe at least one person died at the scene [...] We were lucky enough to be on the front of the tram and so didn't get any injuries. It was a pretty horrific scene, and seeing a teenager pass away in front of you is hard to forget [...] Trams it seems have a lot of momentum [...] This all happened on 29 May 2007 in Krakow, Poland. We took the 79 from the camp ground we were staying at into the city, and it derailed along the way. I believe from how the tram jolted, that the driver was going too fast round a 90 degree corner, and being eastern Europe, the trams and tracks probably are not maintained that well.'

PORTUGAL

Lisbon, 29 May 2011

A collision involving tram No. 553 and a motor vehicle in Lisbon on 29 May 2011. Flickr user PH4.27 says, 'I suspect the car had been parked on the side of the road and the tram driver had estimated the clearance a bit wrong.' (*Photograph courtesy of PH4.27 Photography*)

ROMANIA

Depou Gara, Lasi, 28 August 1996
Collision damage sustained by vehicle No. 228 in Depou Gara, Lasi, on 28 August 1996.
(*Photograph courtesy of Rene Van Lier*)

SERBIA

Ulice Nemanjina/Ulice Hajduk Veljkov, Belgrade, 25 May 2006
Photographer Rene Van Lier, who took this picture on 25 May 2006, states, 'I was just walking
when the collision happened. This is a classical crash. A car is turning to left (in this case not
allowed on this crossing) without [the driver] watching if there is a tram [approaching].'

SWITZERLAND

Geneva, 16 June 2006

A tram derailed on Friday 16 June 2006 on the Boulevard Georges Favon, near Route du Stand, Geneva, causing major traffic jams. The incident caused three light casualties. It was reported that sometime after 3.42 p.m., amazed eyewitnesses saw the tram travel 30 metres across the road, then up the sidewalk. It came, at the closest, to within 30 cm of a shop window. According to Raymond Wicky, head of the Service d'incendie et de secours (SIS; Fire and Help services), the three casualties suffered from whiplash injuries to the neck and back. The driver suffered shock, as did several shop owners. Nine fire engines, two ambulances, and a dozen policemen and cars quickly arrived at the scene.

Geneva, 8 April 1978

Derailment in Council-General at 10.00 a.m. Saturday 8 April 1978, involving motor and trailer 721 301 and 718 motor and trailer 304. (*Photograph courtesy of Trams to the Son*)

UNITED STATES

San Francisco, 23 June 2007

Photographer Dean Barrow states that on his first tram ride through San Francisco on 23 June 2007, he came across this small mishap. He also added, 'The tram was the Fisherman's Wharf line running from the hotel I was staying at called Holiday Inn Golden Gateway. As far as I could tell no one was injured, it was a spur of a moment picture as we were passing by on the adjacent track.'

San Francisco, 3 August 2009

Kay Unck read about this accident on the SF online newspaper and drove to the scene after work, parked, walked a few blocks and took some photographs. The streetcars and the vehicle involved in the accident on Monday 3 August 2009 were all travelling west, or outbound, on Market Street near Noe Street. Witnesses said the driver of a historic orange streetcar from Milan was talking to a passenger when he suddenly slammed on the brakes. The streetcar hit a silver Nissan Pathfinder, sending several people tumbling to the floor of the car. The Pathfinder was pushed against a maroon-coloured streetcar, crushing the front and back of the car, but leaving the middle intact. Two people were seen exiting the vehicle. The driver of the streetcar and the driver of the Pathfinder were transported to a hospital for treatment, but the injuries did not appear to be serious. Three other people were treated at the scene for minor injuries, and one person refused treatment.